The Big Little Devotional Guide

AMAZING ME

Little
WORSHIP
Company

With thanks to Tim Dobson, Sarah Joy, Colse Leung, Rachel Noyce, Jo Sunderland and Jenny Sykes.

Additional images by Sarah Joy, Ramsey Selim, Jo Sunderland and Shutterstock.

Contents

Little WORSHIP Company

Discovering GOD together

At **Little Worship Company**, our heart is to inspire and delight children with a knowledge of God, and to support them as they begin to take their first steps of faith. We also want to help parents as they walk with their children on this wonderful journey. Our range of beautifully-crafted, Biblically-based resources have been designed with the whole family in mind, so that all God's children, little ones and bigger ones, can discover more of God and His incredible love together.

There are four stunning DVDs that make up **Little Worship Company** Series 1:

- **Amazing Me**
- **Beautiful World**
- Praise Party
- **Wonderful Day**

This devotional guide has been written for use alongside the **Little Worship Company: Amazing Me** DVD. In this book, you and your family are invited to journey with our hosts, Hal and Mr. and Mrs. Looyah, as they explore what it means to know God and live for Him together.

Welcome to Amazing Me!

We are all God's children, made and loved by our Heavenly Father. In **Little Worship Company: Amazing Me** Devotional Guide, you'll explore how special we are – discovering not only the amazing people we were made to be, but the even *more* amazing God who invites us to be His friends.

How to use this resource

To make the most of this resource, choose a time of the day or week which suits you and your family. It might be just before bed, just after lunch or sometime over the weekend.

- **Watch a chapter from the DVD.** Each chapter will include a short slot from Hal and a worship song.

- **Read through the accompanying Bible verse** and short, family-friendly reflection, found in this devotional guide.

- **As a family, talk through the discussion question together.** Close with the short prayer found at the bottom of the page.

Each reflection includes a simple craft or recipe suggestion to go with it. You could do this as part of the reflection, or at another time to remind you of some of the ideas you've been exploring.

What else is in this resource?

As well as all-age devotions, you'll find a little 'big' thought that draws on the same themes but is aimed specifically at adults. Each one includes suggestions for further reflection and a short prayer. This could be something you reflect on while your child engages in the craft, or you might choose to read it over a cup of tea, by yourself, later on.

At **Little Worship Company**, we want to provide you with practical ideas for making your faith part of family life. In this book, you'll find some of our best tips for engaging with God daily **(page 23)** and ideas for developing 'holy habits' with your family **(page 37)**.

Old or young, big or small –
every single one of us is precious to God!

You'll probably spot a few LOVE BUGS on our pages. They might be little – but they remind us of God's BIG love for us.

Amazing Me

1 God made me

Psalm 139:13-14 (LWC)

You created **every** single tiny bit of me. You put me **together** in my mummy's tummy. **Thank you God.** I am **brilliantly** and **marvellously** made.

Wow! Did God really make me?

Yes, Hal, He did. He made you and He knows you inside and out!

Have you ever seen a mummy with a baby in her tummy? You can't really see the baby – just a bump which the baby snuggles inside! But the Bible says that God has always seen us and always known us – even before we were born! In fact, the Bible says that God is the one who made us. He put us together, like an artist making an amazing piece of art.

He knows every single thing about you. The colour of your eyes and your hair, the things you are really good at, even the things that make you laugh and cry – He made and knows it all. You are God's special creation – **His fantastic, one-of-a-kind work of art!**

TALK TOGETHER

Talk about all the things which make you one of a kind. Say thank you to God for them!

MAKE TOGETHER

You are God's work of art. Take some play dough. You might like to make a little person, or a collection of people, like your family and friends. As you do it, think about how God carefully made you – and smiled as He did so! Model a little heart and put it in the middle of your play-dough people to show how much God loves you!

PRAY TOGETHER

Dear God, **thank you that I am one of Your amazing ideas!** Thank you that You know every single part of me and that I am incredibly special to You. **Amen.**

Amazing Me

TIME TO REFLECT

Psalm 139:13-18

For you created my inmost being; you knit me together in my mother's womb.

I praise you because I am fearfully and wonderfully made;

your works are wonderful, I know that full well.

My frame was not hidden from you when I was made in the secret place,

when I was woven together in the depths of the earth.

Your eyes saw my unformed body; all the days ordained for me

were written in your book before one of them came to be.

How precious to me are your thoughts, God! How vast is the sum of them!

Were I to count them, they would outnumber the grains of sand –

when I awake, I am still with you.

"In the beginning, God created…" These are the very first words in the Bible and they set the tone for the rest of Scripture. God is the author of life, the first and last, Alpha and Omega. He is inextricably linked to all created things – and that includes us. This magnificent psalm is all about how our lives, our very selves, are intimately bound up in God. Whether we feel it or not – even whether we choose it or not! Our lives have been in God's hands from the moment we were conceived. And they still are. There is no place we can go which is beyond His reach. There is no part of us which is beyond His understanding. He knows our secret thoughts, our hopes and

fears, our joys and sorrows too – and He is with us in all of it.

THIS PSALM OVERFLOWS WITH JOY AND THANKSGIVING – AND WITH GOOD REASON.

We can find freedom in being known and held by the God who made us. As parents, we can be encouraged that this is true for our children too. There are no words to describe seeing your child face-to-face for the first time, or what it's like to watch them grow and to discover their emerging personalities. But there is so much we don't know about them yet – which can bring excitement and fear in equal measure! But God knows them. They are His own precious creation. He has them in His hands, just as He has us in His hands. And we can be completely confident that He will not let any of us go.

TIME TO ACT

1   Read the following words from Psalm 139:14:
I praise you because I am fearfully and wonderfully made.

Read them several times, emphasising each of the words in turn, for example:

I *praise you because I am fearfully and wonderfully made.*

*I **praise** you because I am fearfully and wonderfully made.*

*I praise **you** because I am fearfully and wonderfully made.*

What might God be saying to you through this?

2   Look back over any pictures you've collected of your child(ren), from their earliest days until now. As you look at them, reflect on God's perfect knowledge of you and your family and commit yourselves to Him.

TIME TO PRAY

I praise you, God, because You have known and loved me from the very beginning of my life.

Thank you that Your hands are big enough to hold me, my family and every single person in this world, and that we can trust You completely.

Amen.

ONLY GOT A MINUTE?

- God is the author of life, the first and the last.
- Our lives have been in God's hands from the moment we were conceived. He still holds us.
- God holds our children, just as He holds us.
- He will not let us go.

Amazing Me

1 Peter 2:9 (LWC)

I am God's very special treasure.

God made me – I'm His amazing work of art!

Yes you are, Hal. But not only that. God LOVES YOU too – more than you could ever imagine!

What is your number one, most favourite thing in the world? A teddy? A toy train? A blanket? Maybe it's your family? We all have something that we like to keep close to us – something that's really special to us. And God does too. **You!**

The Bible says that you are God's special treasure. He made you, He knows you, and **He really, really loves you!** In fact, there's nothing in the world more precious to Him than you. The Bible calls God our amazing Heavenly dad who is always beside us. He carries us when we get tired. He hugs us when we feel sad. And there's nothing in the world that can ever stop Him from loving us.

TALK TOGETHER

Collect up your most special things. Take some time to play with them. Or maybe have a big cuddle with your mum or dad! How does it make you feel? Think about how God feels the same way about you – but even more!

MAKE TOGETHER

You are God's precious child. Make a finger puppet family using pipe cleaners, pom-poms for the heads and googly eyes. Think about how you are part of God's family, loved by an amazing Heavenly Father!

PRAY TOGETHER

Dear God, **thank you that I am Your special treasure** and You are my Big Heavenly Dad. Thank you that You are with me and that You love me more than I will ever know. **Amen.**

Amazing Me

TIME TO REFLECT

John 1:1-13

In the beginning was the Word, and the Word was with God, and the Word was God. He was with God in the beginning. Through him all things were made; without him nothing was made that has been made. In him was life, and that life was the light of all mankind. The light shines in the darkness, and the darkness has not overcome it.

There was a man sent from God whose name was John. He came as a witness to testify concerning that light, so that through him all might believe. He himself was not the light; he came only as a witness to the light.

The true light that gives light to everyone was coming into the world. He was in the world, and though the world was made through him, the world did not recognize him. He came to that which was his own, but his own did not receive him. Yet to all who did receive him, to those who believed in his name, he gave the right to become children of God – children born not of natural descent, nor of human decision or a husband's will, but born of God.

It's said that an eminent theologian was once asked what was the most important lesson He'd learned over the years. His answer was simple:

"JESUS LOVES ME – THIS I KNOW, FOR THE BIBLE TELLS ME SO."

One of the big themes that runs through Scripture is God's incredible love for the world He created. And that love is supremely expressed in Jesus. It's often said that something is worth what somebody is willing to pay for it. We know how precious we are to God because He was willing to send His Son to die for us – to deal, once and for all, with the sin that separated us from Him and to welcome us into His family. Yes, Jesus loves us. The cross proves it.

Becoming a parent teaches you new lessons in love. You discover what it means to give happily and forgive readily, to rejoice in the hugs and little expressions of love, and to sacrifice without counting the cost. As we learn, first-hand, what it means to love like this, let's not forget that we, too, are children of a Heavenly Father, dearly beloved by the One who initiated and perfected it. This news is almost too wonderful to grasp. There are so many pictures that Scripture uses for God – Creator, Judge, Master. But God's heart is that we know Him intimately, as we know a parent. The love we have for our children helps us understand His love for us, but it still falls short. God really delights in us – despite our weaknesses and failings. He doesn't run out of patience when we get it wrong. And He is always at hand to help us – we only need to ask!

TIME TO ACT

1   When are the times you need to be reassured of how precious you are to God? Take some time to meditate on the words of this hymn:

How deep the Father's love for us
How vast – beyond all measure –
That He should give His only Son
To make a wretch His treasure.

Stuart Townend © *1995 Thankyou Music*

2   How have you changed since becoming a parent? How has your relationship with God changed since becoming a parent?

Take some time to read and reflect on 1 John 3:1:

See what great love the Father has lavished on us, that we should be called children of God! And that is what we are!

Think about what you long to be for your children; and consider how God is all of this and more to them, and to you too.

TIME TO PRAY

Thank you, God,
that even though I am
fully grown, I am still
Your child.

May I learn to be loved
by You, and love like You
in turn.

Amen.

60 SECONDS

ONLY GOT A MINUTE?

- God loves the world He created.

- We are so precious to God.

- The love we have for our children helps us begin to understand God's love for us – but His love for us is deeper, bigger and perfect.

- God delights in us, despite our weaknesses and failings.

- God's love never runs out.

BIG

DEVOTION 2 SPARKLING EYES

Amazing Me

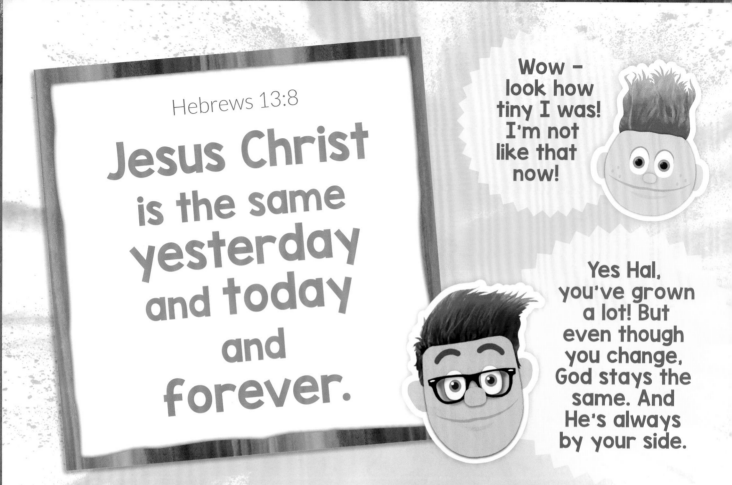

Hebrews 13:8

Jesus Christ is the same yesterday and today and forever.

Wow – look how tiny I was! I'm not like that now!

Yes Hal, you've grown a lot! But even though you change, God stays the same. And He's always by your side.

Do you remember what you were like as a baby? You gurgled and babbled. You wiggled your arms and waggled your feet. You played with rattles and baby toys. But now you are bigger. And you are so different. You can use lots of grown up words. You don't have a rattle any more – you play with bigger children's toys now. Maybe you can ride a bike, or even write your name!

You will change a lot as you grow. But even though you change, God doesn't. The Bible says that God is the same, every day and for evermore. This means that we can completely trust His promises to us. Because He doesn't change, **we know that God will always be with us and always, always love us!**

TALK TOGETHER

God will always be our friend. What do you think makes somebody a good friend? How is God a good friend to us?

MAKE TOGETHER

We might change, but God always stays the same. Make a clock out of a paper plate, a couple of cardboard hands and a paper fastener. A grown-up can help you to write the numbers on it or you can use stickers. Remember that, as time goes by, God will always be there for you.

PRAY TOGETHER

Dear God, **thank you that even though I will change, You never will.** Thank you that You will be with me as I grow and that You will always be my best friend. **Amen.**

Amazing Me

TIME TO REFLECT

Hebrews 13:8

Jesus Christ is the same yesterday and today and forever.

Is there a crazier time of life than when you become a parent? There are so many pressing demands, twenty-four hours a day, seven days a week. No two days are the same. You're in a constant state of flux, with routines changing from one week to the next. In fact, everything seems to be changing. Our core sense of identity and purpose changes dramatically. We become this brand-new person, 'Mummy' or 'Daddy' – something that is both a huge privilege and a huge responsibility! And during this particularly intense season, our walk with God may also change. We may find we struggle to connect with God in the ways we used to. Regular quiet times and church in the sanctuary (rather than the crèche) are not always possible. When our lives are so bound up with our children and their needs, creating dedicated space for God becomes a real challenge.

AS EVERYTHING AROUND US CHANGES, IT'S ENCOURAGING TO REMEMBER THAT GOD NEVER WILL.

His love for us is never in question, based as it is on His perfect nature rather than our imperfect devotion. And His plans, purposes and promises are just as unchanging. As new parents we can sometimes feel a bit lost – personally and spiritually. But the eternal, unchanging God is doing a new thing. He is always opening new ways of encountering Him and His goodness, providing new opportunities to serve and glorify Him. This busy season of early parenthood is like nothing else. But we can be confident that God is as present in our lives now as He ever was, walking beside us and leading us forward.

TIME TO ACT

1 Think about all the different ways you encountered God before you had children. Do you find it easy or difficult to do this now you are a parent? Ask God to show you new opportunities and rhythms for connecting with Him daily during this busy season.

2 We need to be intentional about spending time with the people we love – including God! Book a few hours in the diary to have some 'soul space' – whether that's through a long prayer walk or run, reading the Bible or going to a worship event. If finding childcare is difficult, why not consider setting up a child-minding triplet within your church and taking it in turns?

TIME TO PRAY

Thank you, Father, that even though we may change, You are always the same.

In all the busyness of my life right now, help me to see You more clearly, love You more dearly and follow You more nearly each and every day.

Amen.

ONLY GOT A MINUTE?

- As everything around us changes, it's encouraging to remember that God never will.

- His plans, purposes and promises are unchanging.

- God is offering us new ways to encounter Him. Look for them.

- Be confident that God is as present in our lives now as He ever was, walking beside us and leading us forward.

Amazing Me

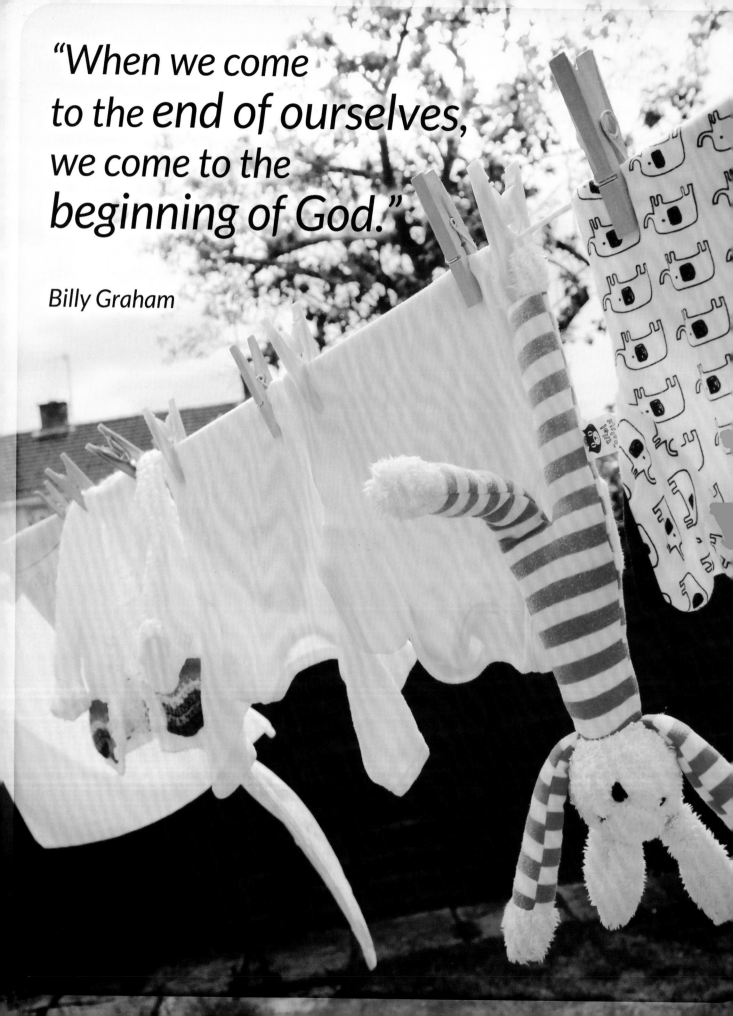

"When we come to the end of ourselves, we come to the beginning of God."

Billy Graham

Draw near to God
THE BUSY PARENT'S GUIDE TO CONNECTING WITH GOD

Life with small children is incredibly busy. And that's putting it mildly. It can be difficult to find space for God when you're faced with a thousand pressing demands from the moment you wake up to last thing at night. (And, if your kids don't sleep, throughout the night as well!) But God is never far away. Some of these ideas might help you to become aware of Him with you, even on the busiest days.

- **Have conversations with God.** You might think of Him walking beside you as you push a buggy or sitting beside you at the office. Take a moment to talk over anything that's on your mind. Picture Jesus sitting with you and your family at the dinner table. What conversation would you like to have with Him? How would He include all the family?

- **Say thank you often.** Being thankful for all we've been given increases our awareness of the One who gives it. Whether it's the sight of blossom in spring, or a safe journey, give thanks to God throughout the day.

- **Mind the 'gaps'.** It's possible to combine daily, routine tasks with opportunities to connect with God. Play and sing worship songs around the house. Listen to audio versions of the Bible in the car. Play a study podcast while you prep the vegetables. Sing worship songs or whisper Bible verses over your children as you settle them to sleep.

- **Pray through the chores.** Many of the things we do each day can remind us of God's work in our lives. Pray for your children as you sort their laundry. Thank God for His forgiveness as you clean up messy plates and worktops. Remember how God promises to work all things together for good every time you compost your vegetable waste.

- **Make space for silence.** Sometimes all we need is time to rest. Even if it's just once a day, invest five minutes in doing nothing. Let the next urgent thing wait and find God's peace in the midst of the busyness.

- **Journal.** Keep a record of any 'God' words people have said or given to you, or places where You've experienced His goodness. Look back over it regularly and use it to praise God. Why not do this as a family?

- **Get appy.** With all this technology literally at our fingertips, why not use it to connect with God? Download Bible-reading apps, or apps that will help you pray. Use them when you have a spare minute.

- **Keep an eye on God's promises.** Stick up God's promises or favourite Bible verses around the house. Why not turn the fridge into a prayer-and-promise-wall?

- **Get out more.** Walking gives you space to think – as well as a chance to enjoy God's beautiful world. Why not go on a 'wonder walk' with your family? What will you see to make you say "wow"?

Amazing Me

> ## 1 Timothy 4:12 (MSG)
>
> ## Don't let anyone put you down because you're young.

When will I be old enough to be God's friend? When I'm eight? Or maybe twelve?

Oh, Hal! You're never too young to know God! You can be friends with Him right now!

"You can't go on the zipwire. You're too small!"

"You can't go in the big pool. You're too small!"

"You can't go to school. You're too small!"

It's true that you might be too small for some things. But there's one thing you're never too little for: being God's friend!

The Bible is full of examples of God asking children to be His friends – like Samuel in the Old Testament and the little boy with his packed lunch in the New Testament. And Jesus always, always had time to talk to children! That's because you might be small, but you are incredibly important to God. **And you're never too young to learn how to listen to God and follow Him.**

TALK TOGETHER

If you have a children's Bible, **look up the story of God calling Samuel** and read it together (it can be found in 1 Samuel 3:1-10). Can you imagine how Samuel felt? How can we hear God speaking to us?

MAKE TOGETHER

You are so special to God! Make a crown out of cardboard and sparkly jewel stickers. Thank God that you are a very important person to Him!

PRAY TOGETHER

Dear God, **thank you that I am never too small to be Your friend!** Help me to keep my eyes open to see You, and my ears open to hear what You are asking me to do. **Amen.**

Amazing Me

TIME TO REFLECT

1 Samuel 3:1-10

The boy Samuel ministered before the Lord under Eli. In those days the word of the Lord was rare; there were not many visions. One night Eli, whose eyes were becoming so weak that he could barely see, was lying down in his usual place. The lamp of God had not yet gone out, and Samuel was lying down in the house of the Lord, where the ark of God was.

Then the Lord called Samuel. Samuel answered, "Here I am."
And he ran to Eli and said, "Here I am; you called me."
But Eli said, "I did not call; go back and lie down." So he went and lay down.

Again the Lord called, "Samuel!"
And Samuel got up and went to Eli and said, "Here I am; you called me."
"My son," Eli said, "I did not call; go back and lie down."

Now Samuel did not yet know the Lord: the word of the Lord had not yet been revealed to him.

A third time the Lord called, "Samuel!"
And Samuel got up and went to Eli and said, "Here I am; you called me."
Then Eli realised that the Lord was calling the boy. So Eli told Samuel,
"Go and lie down, and if he calls you, say, 'Speak, Lord, for your servant is listening.'"
So Samuel went and lay down in his place. The Lord came and stood there, calling as at the other times,
"Samuel! Samuel!" Then Samuel said, "Speak, for your servant is listening."

This season of early parenthood opens up new possibilities of encountering God. It also opens up new opportunities for serving God. Parenting is itself a tremendous ministry given by God. He has entrusted you with a wonderful child that He made and loves. This child will encounter that love – initially – through you. From providing food, warmth and shelter, to showering smiles and kisses on your little one, you are – for now – the human face of God's care and provision. But, as well as meeting our child's physical and emotional needs in these early, formative years, we are invited to support our child's spiritual needs too, by helping them discern God's presence in their lives.

As parents we may hope and pray that our children will know and love God as they grow older. But how often do we think about them having a spiritual life now?

DO WE SEE HOW GOD IS ALREADY AT WORK IN OUR CHILDREN?

The Bible makes it clear that age is no barrier to knowing God and being used by Him. In the Old Testament, Samuel is called to an important priestly ministry as a mere child. Paul's instructions to Timothy show how he has complete faith in his (much younger) colleague to continue an important ministry amongst the church in Ephesus while he's away. Our children are never too young to walk with God. But they will need our help as they take their first steps on the journey. Like the priest Eli, we need to be alert to what God is doing, so we can help our children to recognise God as He calls to them.

TIME TO ACT

1 As you pray for your children, ask that God will help you to discern ways in which He is speaking to and leading your children.

2 We can encourage our children to walk with God for themselves by developing 'holy habits'. Think about how you build in prayer, Bible study and worship at home, so that God is not seen as belonging to Sunday but with you in your everyday lives.

TIME TO PRAY

Thank you, God,
that You love my child even more than I do,
and that you have tremendous plans for them.

Help me to see what You are doing in their life already and who You are shaping them to be.

Amen.

60 SECONDS

BIG

ONLY GOT A MINUTE?

- Parenting is a God-given ministry.

- Our children are never too young to walk with God.

- We can help our children to take their first steps on their faith journey.

- How can you build prayer, Bible study and worship with your child into your everyday routine?

Amazing Me

Ephesians 2:10 (LWC)

We are God's best artwork!

Wow! God made me!

That's right, Hal. And He knows exactly what you were made for: an amazing adventure with Him!

Birds were made to fly. Fish were made to swim. Cars were made to take people to exciting places. And ice cream was made to taste delicious on a sunny day. All kinds of wonderful things have been made to do all kinds of wonderful stuff. And we were too!

The Bible says that we are God's marvellous invention. He made us to do amazing things for Him – things that will change the world! We can find out about God's big ideas for us in the Bible. It's God's special instruction book for our life. We might not know exactly what God has planned for us as we get bigger, but if we look in the Bible we'll know which way to go!

TALK TOGETHER

What are your favourite inventions? What would you like to invent? Think about the kinds of things God created us to do – for example, helping other people.

MAKE TOGETHER

God has made you for an amazing adventure with Him! Make a pair of binoculars out of a couple of empty kitchen rolls, sticky tape and string or ribbon. To decorate them, wrap them with wool, paint them, use wrapping paper or add stickers. As you look through them, remember that God shows us the best way to go!

PRAY TOGETHER

Dear God, **thank you that You made me and that You really, really love what You made!** I can't wait to find out what You have planned for me! **Amen.**

Amazing Me

TIME TO REFLECT

Ephesians 2:1-10

As for you, you were dead in your transgressions and sins, in which you used to live when you followed the ways of this world and of the ruler of the kingdom of the air, the spirit who is now at work in those who are disobedient. All of us also lived among them at one time, gratifying the cravings of our flesh and following its desires and thoughts. Like the rest, we were by nature deserving of wrath. But because of his great love for us, God, who is rich in mercy, made us alive with Christ even when we were dead in transgressions – it is by grace you have been saved. And God raised us up with Christ and seated us with him in the heavenly realms in Christ Jesus, in order that in the coming ages he might show the incomparable riches of his grace, expressed in his kindness to us in Christ Jesus. For it is by grace you have been saved, through faith – and this is not from yourselves, it is the gift of God – not by works, so that no one can boast. For we are God's handiwork, created in Christ Jesus to do good works, which God prepared in advance for us to do.

God made us. But He is also *remaking us.* The Bible teaches that we are not functioning fully as the Maker intended. And the reason for this is our sin. Just as a virus infects and devastates a program, so sin has infected our human nature, marring God's wonderful design. But God has a remedy: Jesus. His death destroyed the power of sin, and now God is working in us to restore us to all He originally planned. If we want to know what this looks like – again, Jesus provides the answer. Jesus embodied all that God has in mind for us – the perfect template of humanity. And now, by His Spirit, God is patiently transforming every part of us to be more like Him – from our inner life (our thoughts and attitudes) to our outer actions.

AS PARENTS, WE WANT THE VERY BEST FOR OUR CHILDREN. AND THE BEST LOOKS LIKE JESUS.

Jesus lies at the heart of everything God has for us and wants to do in us. One of the greatest things we can ever do for our kids is to introduce them to Jesus. We can do this by sharing His stories – of His life, death and resurrection. But the most important thing we can do is inspire a love for Him. To show them what it means to follow Him by living out the values He taught – of trust in God, generosity and love without boundaries. So much of what our children learn is 'caught' not 'taught'. And there is nothing more compelling for our children than our own hearts fully alive and open to all God is calling us to in Christ.

TIME TO ACT

1   We are God's amazing work of art – a masterpiece that He is still sculpting and shaping as we submit our lives to Him. Take some time to commit yourself to God again. Know that His Spirit is in you, guiding you and helping you to become more like Jesus.

2   As parents, we want the very best for our children. The best, ultimately, is to place Jesus front and centre of our home lives and to live for Him together. How will you demonstrate what it means to love Jesus – in the things you say and the things you do?

TIME TO PRAY

Thank you, God,
that I am your handiwork.

Thank you that by Your Spirit You are making me more like Jesus.

May You truly be Lord of my life and let me model that to my family.

Amen.

60 SECONDS

ONLY GOT A MINUTE?

- God made us. But He is also *remaking* us.

- By His Spirit, God is patiently transforming every part of us to be more like Him.

- To inspire our children and to introduce them to Jesus, we need to model our own love for God.

- How can you demonstrate what it means to love Jesus, in the things you say and the things you do?

Amazing Me

Zephaniah 3:17

He will take great delight in you... He will **rejoice** over you with **singing.**

I really want to make God happy! But I know I don't always get it right.

Hal, God's love for you is SO big! Nothing will ever change how much He cares for you.

Think about your favourite toy. What would you do if it went missing? You'd look for it, of course! Under the bed, in cupboards, behind the sofa. You'd search everywhere. And when you found it? You'd be so happy! You'd jump and cheer. Maybe you'd do a jiggly, wiggly dance!

Sometimes, it's like we walk away from God. We don't listen to Him, or we make choices that upset Him or other people. And that makes God sad. But no matter what we do, He loves us just the same. He's so happy when we come back to Him and say sorry – just like you're happy when you find a missing toy! In fact, the Bible says **He's so excited that He sings a song over us to celebrate!**

TALK TOGETHER

It's not always easy saying sorry, but it's a really important thing to do. When are the times you need to say sorry to God or to other people?

MAKE TOGETHER

Nothing will ever stop God from loving us. Make a 'love bug' stained-glass window out of sheets of sticky-back plastic and little squares of tissue paper. Stick the tissue paper onto a sheet of plastic, then stick another sheet over the top. Cut it into the shape of a 'love bug' and stick it onto a window. When the sun shines through it, remember how much God loves you!

PRAY TOGETHER

Dear God, **I'm really sorry for the times I make bad choices.** Thank you that I'm Your precious child, and that there's nothing in the world that stops You from loving me. **Amen.**

DEVOTION 6 YOU'RE BEAUTIFUL

Amazing Me

TIME TO REFLECT

Zephaniah 3:14-17

Sing, Daughter Zion; shout aloud, Israel!
Be glad and rejoice with all your heart, Daughter Jerusalem!

The Lord has taken away your punishment, he has turned back your enemy.
The Lord, the King of Israel, is with you; never again will you fear any harm.

On that day they will say to Jerusalem, "Do not fear, Zion; do not let your hands hang limp.
The Lord your God is with you, the Mighty Warrior who saves. He will take great delight in you;
in his love he will no longer rebuke you, but will rejoice over you with singing."

Is there a more beautiful picture than that of our Heavenly Father singing over His children? And yet this promise of tender, wonderful love is bigger than we can imagine. It comes towards the end of Zephaniah – a prophetic book painting God's people at their most rebellious and hard-hearted. They have done absolutely nothing to deserve God's love – and instead everything to deserve His punishment. Yet God opens the way to find His forgiveness, a way back into relationship with Him. And this is our story too. We don't deserve God's love. Our sin makes us unworthy. But the good news of the gospel is that God's love is bigger than our sin. In Jesus, God provided a way to receive His forgiveness. God's Son took our punishment, so that we could become sons and daughters in turn.

As we get older, we perhaps become more aware of our sinfulness – that we don't live up to our own standards, let alone God's. As parents, this sense is often heightened. We have high hopes of what kind of parent we will be. But every hasty word or impatient reaction shows us our shortcomings in high definition.

IT IS ENCOURAGING TO REMEMBER THAT WE ARE NOT DEFINED BY OUR SIN, BUT BY THE GRACE OF GOD.

He doesn't give up on us. His love never runs out. His mercies are new every morning. And when we truly discover God's incredible love for us, we will see grace at work in our lives and relationships. It's only as we humbly encounter God's forgiveness, kindness and patience with us that we find ourselves becoming more forgiving, kind and patient in turn.

TIME TO ACT

1 Reflect on this verse from 1 John:

This is the kind of love we are talking about – not that we once upon a time loved God, but that he loved us and sent his Son as a sacrifice to clear away our sins and the damage they've done to our relationship with God.

1 John 4:10 (The Message)

Take some time to confess to God. Unburden your heart of all your weaknesses and failings. Know that He rejoices in you and receive His forgiveness and grace.

2 Our lives are defined by God's grace. How can we demonstrate that grace in our homes and communities? What does it mean to model the grace of God in the way we speak about each other? And in our actions towards each other?

TIME TO PRAY

Search me, O God, and know my heart.

See if there is any offensive way in me, and lead me in the way everlasting.

Amen.

(Based on Psalm 139:23-24)

ONLY GOT A MINUTE?

- God's love is bigger than our sin and unworthiness.

- Through Jesus, God has created a way to forgive us and to take away our punishment.

- This means we are now children of God!

- When we are not perfect parents, remember that we are not defined by our own shortcomings, but by God's grace.

- God doesn't give up on us – His love never runs out.

Amazing Me

"Point your kids in the right direction..."

Proverbs 22:6 (MSG)

DEVELOPING HOLY HABITS AS A FAMILY

It's amazing the things we can remember from our childhood. The things we hear and the things we do stay with us for the rest of our lives. As parents, we want our children to encounter God. And we have an incredibly important role in helping them to do this. Why not have a go at developing some of these 'holy habits' in your home?

- **Discover Jesus together.** Take time regularly to explore the gospel stories with your children. As you read them, talk about what Jesus is like. What lessons can we learn *about* Him? What can we learn *from* Him?

- **Give thanks regularly.** Light a candle for each person at the dinner table and encourage them to find something to say thank you for. Create a 'thankfulness jar'. When you've done something fun, write or draw what happened. Remember the great times together. Use the jar as an opportunity to praise God.

- **Introduce the dinner-time 'high/low'.** Name one thing from your day that was a 'high' and one thing that was a 'low'. Thank God for the 'highs' and pray for the 'lows'.

- **Plan to pray.** It can be difficult to know what to pray when you're on the spot! Why not make a family prayer schedule? On Mondays pray for cousins, on Tuesdays pray for friends, etc. Use it at mealtimes or bedtimes. Or create a 'prayer hat' that contains different things to pray for. Pull a few things out of the hat each day and pray for them.

- **Build in 'prayer moments'.** Take a minute to say grace at mealtimes. Why not include a 'God bless today' prayer as your children go out to nursery or school?

- **Make time to listen.** Practise 'listening' as well as 'talking' in prayer. Spend a minute lying down in silence to listen to God – then talk about what He said to you.

- **Have a 'Bible board' in the house.** Get a magnet board or a chalkboard. Put up a Bible verse each week – one that will remind you and your family of God's good promises. If your children are a little older, why not see if they can learn it by heart?

- **Talk about your faith.** Faith is caught as much as taught. Share what following God means to you and times God has answered your prayers, so that your children see how your faith impacts you in real life.

- **Be hospitable.** We're called to "practise hospitality" (Romans 12:13). Invite people to join you for a meal or family outing – whether that's your children's friends or an elderly neighbour.

- **Learn generosity.** Research local charities that you could support as a family. Go shopping for food to give to a food bank. Give away toys and clothes that your children have outgrown. Do these things together, so that your children learn how good it feels to give!

Amazing Me

> Joshua 1:9 (LWC)
>
> Be **strong** and be **courageous**. Do not be **afraid** or **troubled**, for the Lord your God is **with you** wherever you go.

I don't always feel amazing. Sometimes I feel scared.

I know, Hal. We all have to do scary things sometimes! But remember – God is right beside you.

What's the biggest, scariest thing you've ever done? Perhaps you learnt to swim or ride a bike. Maybe you started at nursery or school, or moved house. Going somewhere for the first time and making new friends is one of the scariest things we do – even for grown-ups!

God has a big adventure in store for us. As we get bigger, He'll take us to new places and ask us to do new things. We might not always feel good enough or brave enough to do them. But the Bible promises that God is always with us. (Actually, there's nowhere in the world that God isn't!) He's super big and super strong. And because He promises to help us, we can be super-duper-brave!

TALK TOGETHER

Talk about times when you have needed to be brave. Are you facing anything now that you need to be brave for? Talk to God about it!

MAKE TOGETHER

God makes us brave! Create your own superhero costume using an old T-shirt. What will your superhero name be? Remember that God makes us braver than any superhero, because we know He is always with us.

PRAY TOGETHER

Dear God, **thank you that I never need to be scared,** because You're always with me. Thank you that You make me brave! **Amen.**

TIME TO REFLECT

Joshua 1:1-11

After the death of Moses the servant of the Lord, the Lord said to Joshua son of Nun, Moses' aide: "Moses my servant is dead. Now then, you and all these people, get ready to cross the Jordan River into the land I am about to give to them – to the Israelites. I will give you every place where you set your foot, as I promised Moses. Your territory will extend from the desert to Lebanon, and from the great river, the Euphrates – all the Hittite country – to the Mediterranean Sea in the west. No one will be able to stand against you all the days of your life. As I was with Moses, so I will be with you; I will never leave you nor forsake you. Be strong and courageous, because you will lead these people to inherit the land I swore to their ancestors to give them.

"Be strong and very courageous. Be careful to obey all the law my servant Moses gave you; do not turn from it to the right or to the left, that you may be successful wherever you go. Keep this Book of the Law always on your lips; meditate on it day and night, so that you may be careful to do everything written in it. Then you will be prosperous and successful. Have I not commanded you? Be strong and courageous. Do not be afraid; do not be discouraged, for the Lord your God will be with you wherever you go."

So Joshua ordered the officers of the people: "Go through the camp and tell the people, 'Get your provisions ready. Three days from now you will cross the Jordan here to go in and take possession of the land the Lord your God is giving you for your own.'"

Some of the most enduring stories in the Bible are adventure stories. But the heroes are rarely 'heroic'. Joshua leading God's people into the Promised Land is one such story. God made a covenant to Abraham that His descendants would have a land of their own. Moses led his people out of Egypt but went no further than the wilderness. Now, God tells Joshua that the time has come for them to claim their inheritance. Although we don't hear anything from Joshua himself, God's words indicate how he must have been feeling. The command to *"be strong and courageous"* appears three times in this short passage. Clearly Joshua listened to God with a wave of conflicting emotions: excitement that they are about to reach the Promised Land and sheer terror at the magnitude of the task ahead.

LIFE WITH GOD IS AN ADVENTURE.

As parents, we want to show our children what it means to follow where He leads. But truly following God requires courage. The things He asks aren't always easy. We might feel daunted by a lack of experience. Or the task in question might go against the cultural grain. A particular weak spot for us may be our children: will doing this impact negatively on them? But these five simple words in verse 9 – *"Have I not commanded you?"* – are a complete game-changer. When the God of the Universe asks something of us, He gives us His authority to do it. We can find the courage to go ahead. Not because of our own confidence, but because we can trust in God, His perfect commands and His unfailing promises.

TIME TO ACT

1   It's natural to feel fearful in the face of a challenge. The opposite of fear is faith: trusting in who God is and in what He has done. Make a list of the times God has been faithful to you. Keep it close to you. Read it whenever you need to be reminded of God's faithfulness.

2   As parents, we need to model taking steps of faith. Has God been asking you to take a step of faith recently? What has been holding you back? Ask God to open the doors and to give you the courage to walk through them.

TIME TO PRAY

Thank you, God, that I can stand on Your faithful promises and rest in Your perfect will.

Grant me the courage to follow where You lead, now and always.

Amen.

ONLY GOT A MINUTE?

- Life with God is an adventure.

- Sometimes following God requires courage.

- But when the God of the Universe asks something of us, He gives us His authority to do it.

- We can trust in God, in His perfect commands and in His unfailing promises.

- Which doors do you need to walk through? Ask God to give you the courage to walk through them.

Philippians 4:13 (LWC)

I can do anything – Jesus has made me strong!

Thanks for helping me, Mum. I couldn't do it without you!

I love helping you, Hal. And God loves helping us too.

Some things are REALLY heavy! Think about a big box of your favourite toys. Or a suitcase full of clothes. There's no way we can carry these things by ourselves – we're just not strong enough! But the good news is – we don't have to. We have a grown-up around who will come and help us out!

As we get bigger, there might be times when our heart feels heavy. We might sometimes feel sad or worried. But the Bible promises that God is always near and always listening. There's nothing too big or too small for Him. And when we tell Him about it, He gives us His super-strength on the inside. **There's nothing we can't get through when we're with Him!**

TALK TOGETHER

Take some time to talk about anything which might be troubling you. Tell God about it. Ask Him to help you feel strong.

MAKE TOGETHER

God makes us strong. Make some handprints with paint. When they are dry, draw a picture of yourself in the middle to remind you that God carries you in His hands. Make some pictures for your family and friends too.

PRAY TOGETHER

Thank you, God, that **no matter what I go through, You will always help me.** Thank you that You make me strong! **Amen.**

Amazing Me

TIME TO REFLECT

Philippians 4:4-13

Rejoice in the Lord always. I will say it again: Rejoice! Let your gentleness be evident to all. The Lord is near. Do not be anxious about anything, but in every situation, by prayer and petition, with thanksgiving, present your requests to God. And the peace of God, which transcends all understanding, will guard your hearts and your minds in Christ Jesus.

Finally, brothers and sisters, whatever is true, whatever is noble, whatever is right, whatever is pure, whatever is lovely, whatever is admirable – if anything is excellent or praiseworthy – think about such things. Whatever you have learned or received or heard from me, or seen in me – put it into practice. And the God of peace will be with you.

I rejoiced greatly in the Lord that at last you renewed your concern for me. Indeed, you were concerned, but you had no opportunity to show it. I am not saying this because I am in need, for I have learned to be content whatever the circumstances. I know what it is to be in need, and I know what it is to have plenty. I have learned the secret of being content in any and every situation, whether well fed or hungry, whether living in plenty or in want. I can do all this through him who gives me strength.

Life is rarely simple. Whether it's the everyday stresses and strains or more pressing trials and tribulations, life can often feel overwhelming. It is encouraging to remember, then, that large portions of the New Testament were written by people in difficult circumstances to people in similarly pressing situations. Paul wrote his letter to the Philippians during one of his many periods in prison – yet he's able to say with confidence, *"I can do all things through God who strengthens me."* He exudes peace, contentment and strength in all circumstances – even in times of extreme trial. There's a suggestion in verses 4-7 that this is as much a habit as a gift from God. It is the continual practice of trusting God – to provide and to see him safely through – that gives Paul this incredible peace.

We probably know by now that saying "yes" to following God does not guarantee us a trouble-free existence.

WHAT IT DOES PROMISE, THOUGH, IS KNOWING GOD, HIS PEACE AND HIS PRESENCE WITH US THROUGH IT ALL.

At these critical times, His strength becomes our strength. As parents, our instincts are to shield our children from life's difficulties, and there is definitely a place for this. We must exercise our judgment. But one of the greatest lessons we can teach our children is that when the going gets tough – and it will – God is with us, carrying us through it. We have a heavenly Father who loves us and who invites us to cast our burdens onto Him. It is not a sign of weakness to give God the things which we simply can't carry. It's the privilege of being His child.

TIME TO ACT

1   Reflect on these lines from an old hymn:

Oh, what peace we often forfeit!
Oh, what needless pain we bear!
All because we do not carry
everything to God in prayer.

Joseph M. Scriven

What concerns and troubles do you need to hand over to God today? Take them to Him and let His peace – the peace that passes understanding – wash over you.

2   As parents, we need to model what it means to trust in God in all circumstances. Consider your first response when life gets difficult. What place does prayer take? How can we encourage our children to pray with us in tough times?

TIME TO PRAY

Thank you, Father, that You are always with me.

Thank you that You are my strength when I have none of my own.

Help me to know Your peace and Your presence in all seasons and circumstances.

Amen.

60 SECONDS

ONLY GOT A MINUTE?

- Choosing to continually trust God in all circumstances gives us peace when times get tough.

- One of the greatest lessons we can teach our children is that when the going gets tough, God is there with us.

- It is not a sign of weakness to give God the things we can't carry. It's the privilege of being His child.

- What concerns and troubles do you need to hand over to God today? Take them to Him and let His peace fill you.

Amazing Me

Crafts and recipes

DEVOTION 1   PLAY-DOUGH FAMILY WITH HEARTS

How to make play dough:

- 8 tbsp plain flour
- 2 tbsp table salt
- 2 tsp cream of tartar
- 60ml warm water
- Food colouring
- 1 tbsp vegetable oil

1. Mix together in a bowl.

2. Once mixed, tip out onto a lightly flour-dusted surface and knead until smooth.

3. Store in an airtight container in the fridge.

DEVOTION 2

Finger puppet family

DEVOTION 3

Cardboard clock

DEVOTION 4

Cardboard crown

DEVOTION 7   SUPERHERO CAPE

You will need:

- An old T-shirt
- Fabric or marker pens
- Fabric or PVA glue
- Felt

1   Get an adult to cut around the front of the neck of the T-shirt and then down the back sides to make a cape.

2   Decorate with fabric pens or marker pens.

3   Cut shapes out of the felt and stick on.

Why not use kitchen roll tubes to make matching armbands?

DEVOTION 5

Binoculars

DEVOTION 6

Stained-glass window

DEVOTION 8

Handprints

Amazing Me

Amazing Me

thank you prayers

Thank you, God, for making me.

Thank you for my jumping legs.

Thank you for my strong arms.

Thank you for my listening ears.

Thank you for my blinking eyes.

Thank you for my nose that can smell.

Thank you for my full tummy.

Thank you for my cool hair.

Thank you for my HUGE smile.

Thank you, God, for amazing me!

Amen.

Also available from

Little WORSHIP Company

The **Little Worship Company** offers a range of inspiring products, including DVDs, an app **(Little Worship Company World)**, devotionals, curriculums and books. Our products are filled with beautifully-produced worship videos, prayers, games, stories and Bible quotes.

Each DVD follows a devotional journey, teaching your child timeless Bible truths. The DVDs and app have been created to help adults and children to discover God together at home, at church or out in the community.

✉ info@littleworshipcompany.com   𝗳 Littleworshipcompany   ⦿ @littleworshipcompany

Little Worship Company World

Worship anytime, anywhere

Through our digital world, hosted by the entertaining **Looyah family,** you and your child will be taken on a journey through beautifully-produced worship videos, games, stories, Bible quotes and age-appropriate studies. Each week there will be a new exciting journey of content to explore, as you and your little one discover God together.